C000254999

Introduction

Eyam Museum tells the story of life in the village. The aim of this book is to tell you about the brave people who lived and died during the time of the plague. Their stories were told by parents to their children for 200 years and then they were collected in a book, to make sure that they would be remembered for ever.

Contents

Pre-History	4
A Killer Arrives	6
George Viccars	8
A Very Unusual Cure	10
A Sad Tale	12
The Village Rules	14
The Worst Time of All	16
The Gravedigger	18
A Happier Day Arrives	20
Some Plague Cures	22

Written by John Clifford
Illustrated by Les Ives
Published by Colour History Ltd
in association with the Eyam Museum ©2006
13 digit ISBN number 978-0-9552751-3-5

Pre-History

Eyam's story began long before the plague arrived, even before the Saxons who were the first settlers here. They named the village Eyam, meaning village by the water. EY means water in Saxon language and HAM or AM was a village or camp.

Eyam Museum has evidence of people who lived here 2,000 years ago and not far from the village there are remains of an Iron Age Fort. Stone and flint tools have been found dating back to the days of cave dwellers. We cannot show you fossils of dinosaurs, but we know that rhinoceros and other great beasts roamed the hills.

The Romans had a camp a few miles away and mined nearby for lead. If you walk in the hills and fields around the village you can find traces of the old mine workings.

Did you know?
There is a cross, which is now in the Churchyard, which is over 1,000 years old. It was raised outside the village before the people could afford to build a proper church. They would meet at the cross with people from nearby villages to worship the Lord. When the church was built people forgot about the old cross and it was lost for many hundreds of years.

A Killer Arrives

Late in August 1665 a dreadful disease suddenly appeared in the village. People thought it had come from London in materials delivered to Alexander Hadfield, the village tailor. George Viccars, Hadfield's assistant, opened the goods and soon fell ill and died a few days later.

Many people think it was bubonic plague, a disease usually spread by fleas, which lived on rats. Some professors today doubt that it was the plague, but nobody doubts that a killer disease had arrived to cause a terrible time in the village.

In the first three weeks 6 people died, but far worse was to come. In the next month more people died in the village than had done in the whole of the previous year. In the tailor's house alone 3 people died, but the lady next door lost 25 relations! The plague lasted for 14 months and took 260 lives. The disease affected 76 families, about 350 people in all, out of the 160 families of about 800 people who lived in the village.

Did you know?
In London people lit fires in the streets to drive the plague back into the sky. Many men puffed on tobacco pipes hoping for the same protection!

George Viccars

George Viccars, the first victim was a skilled workman. He was a journeyman tailor, who had learned his trade as an apprentice and was now qualified. Journeymen worked for a daily wage. The name comes from a French word journee which means daily. So, he earned a day's wage for a day's work and it does not mean that he travelled.

The disease was caused by a flea bite. One of the signs of the disease was a very painful lump or bubo, usually at the top of the legs, though sometimes it would grow in the arm pit or under the chin. It could grow as big as a small apple. Other people might get the disease in their lungs and they would cough and sneeze. This was far more dangerous, because when people coughed the disease spread quickly without the help of rats and fleas.

It is hard to imagine the pain and horror of this disease; aches, pains and spots. Doctors would look for thirty-three signs of the disease on your body.

Did you know?
People were advised to stay cool, avoid exercise, especially dancing, and not to have a bath! Ladies clutched flowers or herbs to their noses to avoid catching the plague!

A Very Unusual Cure

Plague reached Margaret Blackwell's house and killed her brother Anthony who was ten years old. He was buried on Christmas Eve in 1665. In 1666 her two sisters, father and mother all died and then she fell ill too.

One day as her older brother Francis was making breakfast Margaret called out in pain and after helping her he went back to his meal. He had cooked bacon, which had left a lot of fat in the pan. Francis did not throw it away, but saved it in a clean jug, which he left on the table before going out.

A little later Margaret felt a terrible thirst and without anyone to help her, weak and dizzy with pain, she staggered to the kitchen looking for water. Thinking the milk jug on the table contained milk she drank greedily. The fat must have made her very sick, but she rested for a while and when Francis returned, afraid that his sister may have died whilst he was away, he was amazed to find her alive and feeling much better. Margaret made a full recovery!

Did you know?
The Lord Mayor of London at the time of the plague thought that the disease was carried by cats, and dogs. He ordered that all pet cats, dogs and any wild ones caught roaming the streets should be killed.

A Sad Tale

Emmot Siddall of Eyam and Rowland Torre who lived in the next village were hoping to be married. They delayed their wedding because of the plague, but Rowland often went to see Emmot at her house.

Mrs Siddall told them that it was too dangerous for them to risk their lives by meeting. However, they continued to meet in secret until one day Emmot did not arrive. Again and again Rowland went to meet her, but she never came. Afterwards he found out why...

Emmot had lost her father, a brother and three sisters in six weeks in 1665. A very sad Mrs Siddall married John Daniel in April 1666, but there was very little rejoicing as her beloved Emmott died only five days after the wedding. John Daniel died in July and his new wife died in October. Her last act was to ask her friend to pass Josiah, the only survivor in her family and only three years old, to her friends the Thorpes to look after him, as they had lost all their children.

Question?
Do you think that Emmot might have caught the plague flea from a guest at her mother's wedding? If she has what will happen to her?

The Village Rules

The plague spread quickly as summertime came, but there were no doctors or nurses to help them, so the villagers asked their parson the Rev. William Mompesson to help. He met with the Reverend Thomas Stanley, who had been village parson before Mompesson arrived and they formed a plan which was accepted by the village:-

1st   The Churchyard was to be closed and until the sickness had passed, people were asked to bury their own dead in their gardens or in fields. This was to make sure that they were buried very quickly before others could be infected.

2nd The Church door was to be locked and services held in the open air. Now there was space for families to meet together to worship, but they were far enough away from each other to avoid the risk of catching the plague.

3rd   The village would be 'closed'. If nobody left and nobody came in, the plague could not spread to other places. People outside the village, especially the Earl of Devonshire, supplied food to the village boundary.

These were difficult decisions to reach as the two men were not friends and did not like each other!

The Worst Time of All

Plague is worse in warm weather. In July 1666 there were 56 deaths and in August there were 78. By the end of August there had been a total of 217 plague deaths. Altogether 260 people died of the plague in fourteen months.

Mrs Hancock buried her husband and 6 children in eight days. You can see their graves if you walk up Riley Lane, however their home has long disappeared. Afterwards she went to Sheffield where she joined her grown up son. Although she had been close to the disease she did not carry the germs, but if she had all of Sheffield would have suffered terribly too.

Mrs Mompesson, the parson's wife, died on the last Sunday in August 1666. She is buried in the churchyard and the only person buried there after it was closed. Every year on that same Sunday a wreath of red roses is placed on her grave and a special service to remember those sad days is held outside, close to where Mr Mompesson held his services during the plague.

Did you know?
If you visit Eyam on the last Sunday in August you will see a wreath of roses on Mrs Mompesson's grave. You can join the long procession of people who walk to the site of the service and sing hymns written for this special day.

The Gravedigger

Marshall Howe was a lead miner. He was a strong man and although he did catch the plague he recovered. Sadly his wife and little boy died. Trusting his luck Howe offered to help people who were unable to bury their own dead. He made people hand over some of their possessions as payment to him for digging the graves of their relatives.

One day, after digging a grave for Edward Unwin, he went to collect the body. In those plague days bodies were dragged to their graves by means of a rope, or on a sheet for fear of being too close and catching the plague.

As Howe dragged Unwin's body along, perhaps down the stairs, the 'body' suddenly called out for a drink! Marshall Howe ran from the house in fright leaving Edward Unwin lying on the floor. If he had not called out for a drink Unwin would almost certainly have been buried alive! Marshall Howe did survive and became the village Dog Whipper and began a new life with a new wife.

Did you know?
A Dog Whipper was paid to sit in the church and make sure that dogs were kept out and did not make a mess, or cause a nuisance during the services!

A Happier Day Arrives

A short time after the plague left Eyam, Matthew Morten, whose wife and children had died of the plague, was out walking Flash, his greyhound. Suddenly, Flash ran off towards a lady who was walking towards them. Maybe the dog thought his lost mistress had returned, as he made such a fuss of the stranger.

However, the lady was Sarah Hawksworth who had been married at the start of those terrible days and a year later was a widow. When Morten caught up with his dog he talked to Sarah and they became good friends and eventually they married.

The Latest News

An American doctor, who has studied the plague, believes that today some people have one very special gene, which can protect them from plague. He discovered that this gene is present in families from Eyam who are descendants of plague survivors!

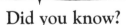

Did you know?
Long ago it was fashionable to wear wigs. Samuel Pepys, a famous person in London at that time, bought a new wig, but dare not wear it in case it had been made from the hair of someone who had died of the plague!

Some Plague Cures

People thought that medicine had to taste nasty to make you better! Some of the medicines used at the time of the plague were really awful and often quite expensive. Here are a few very strange remedies:-

- Swallow the powdered horn of a unicorn.
- Swallow some gold boiled in broth.
- Take a live frog and lay it with its belly next to the plague sore. If the patient is to recover the frog must burst within one hour. (That is because the poison is passing into the frog!) Keep doing this until the frogs no longer burst!
- Some people cut out the swellings from dead patients, dried them and fed them to other sick people!
- One doctor placed a huge dog called a mastiff on the chest of a patient and left it sitting there for four hours!
- Rogues and villains sold a magic cure which might cost a poor person a whole week's wage. This is what they bought printed like this on a small piece of paper:-

A B R A C A D A B R A
A B R A C A D A B R
A B R A C A D A B
A B R A C A D A
A B R A C A D
A B R A C A
A B R A C
A B R A
A B R
A B
A

ABRACADABRA is a well known magic word and written to form a triangle, which is also a magic shape, it was supposed to make powerful magic to cure disease!